ERTÉ

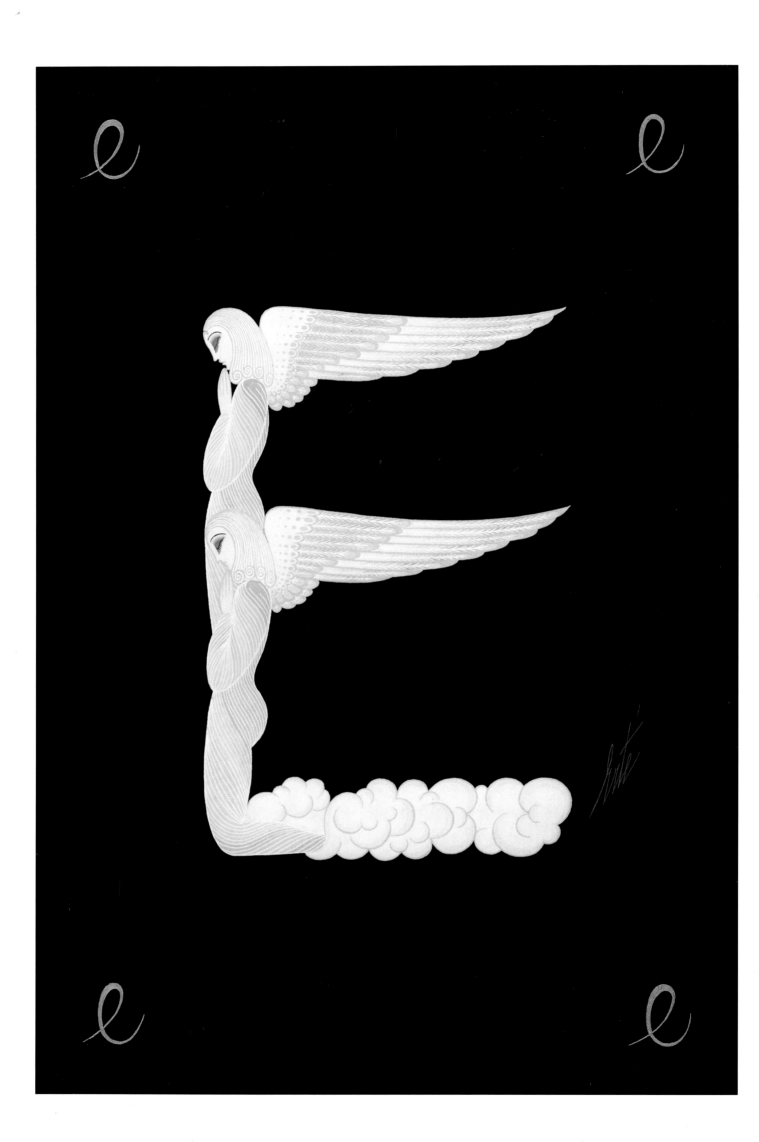

ERTÉ

JEAN TIBBETTS

Grange
BOOKS

Published by Grange Books
An imprint of Grange Books PLC
The Grange
Grange Yard
London SE1 3AG

Produced by Saturn Books
Kiln House, 210 New Kings Road
London SW6 4NZ

ISBN 1 85627 917 0

Printed in China

Reprinted 1996

PAGE 1
Self-Portrait, 1969
Gouache, 11¼ × 8¼ inches
(28.6 × 20.9 cm)

PAGE 2
Letter E from the *Alphabet*
series, 1977
Gouache, 10 × 6½ inches
(25.4 × 16.5 cm)

BELOW
Curtain design for *Madame
Butterfly*, George White's
Scandals, 1926
Gouache, 11¼ × 15¼ inches
(28.6 × 38.7 cm)

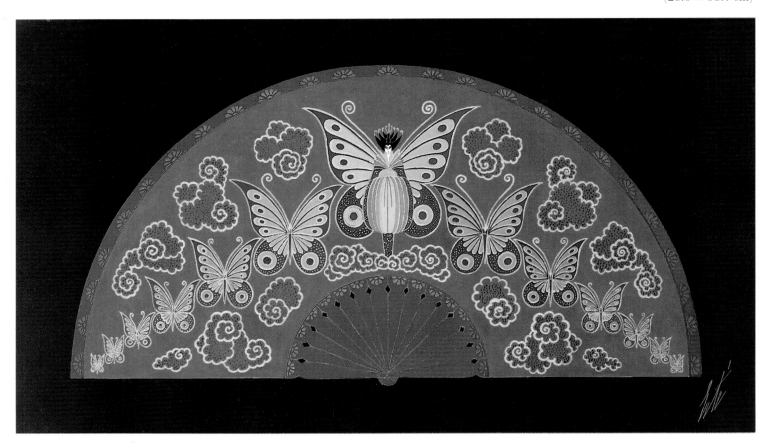

CONTENTS

INTRODUCTION

Early in a career that began in 1912 when he was 19 years old, Romain de Tirtoff, the Russian-born artist who called himself Erté after the French pronunciation of his initials, was regarded as a 'miraculous magician,' whose spectacular fashions transformed the ordinary into the outstanding, whose period costumes made the present vanish mystically into the past, and whose décors converted bare stages into sparkling wonderlands of fun and fancy. When his career ended with his death in 1990, Erté was considered as 'one of the twentieth-century's single most important influences on fashion,' 'a mirror of fashion for 75 years,' and the unchallenged 'prince of the music hall,' who had been accorded the most significant international honors in the field of design and whose work was represented in major museums and private collections throughout the world.

It is not surprising that Erté's imaginative designs for fashion, theater, opera, ballet, music hall, film and commerce achieved such renown, for they are as crisp and innovative in their color and design as they are elegant and extravagant in character, and redolent of the romance of the pre- and post-Great War era, the period when Erté's hand became mature, fully developed and representative of its time. Art historians and scholars define Erté's unique style as transitional Art Deco, because it bridges the visual gap between the *fin-de-siècle* schools of Symbolism, with its ethereal quality, Art Nouveau, with its high ornament, and the mid-1920s movement of Art Deco, with its inspirational sources and concise execution.

In his later years, Erté stated that no contemporary art influenced him, and that, save for elementary courses in drafting, his was a self-taught style that resulted from his exposure to the domestic and Near-Eastern decorative arts that he had enjoyed as a child in Russia. To emphasize this, he often cited his first successful costume design, produced when he was five years old: a modified sarafan, the traditional dress of Little Russia, which his mother later had rendered into reality and wore to a Winter Palace reception.

BELOW FAR LEFT
Green velvet evening coat for
American Houses, 1913

BELOW LEFT
Evening dress for Norio Souzoke,
Collection of Robes, Tokyo, 1975
These two fashion designs from
the beginning and the end of
Erté's career demonstrate the
unchanging fluidity of his line.

RIGHT
Pen and pencil sketch of *Three
Models*, made in 1911, the year
that Erté graduated from
Kronstadt College in St
Petersburg. It is signed 'Tiz,' an
early *nom de plume*.

This artist once confessed that he 'couldn't live without drawing' – even as a toddler – because he 'loved to invent' his personal worlds of wonder. And early in his life that was fine, thought his father, Lieutenant General Piotr Tirtoff (or Tyrtov, depending upon the method of transliteration from Cyrillic script), but the son's passion was irrelevant to the military career that the father had planned for him when he was born on November 23, 1892 in St Petersburg. According to Piotr's plan, his child would be schooled in the basics at home, would study the humanities at school in his pre-teens, and would then enter the Imperial officers' candidate school, to follow his family's footsteps in state service. This was the unflagging professional pattern that every Tirtoff male had undertaken since the twilight of the Golden Horde in the 1540s, when Gavrila, the first Tirtoff to assume that surname, acted as the Tartar ambassador from the Kazan khanate to the Crimea. Respected diplomats and army officers succeeded him on the male side of the Tirtoff line until the reign of Catherine the Great, when the family opted for careers in the Empire's expanding navy – the service of choice for Piotr and, as he expected, for his newborn son.

Yet this plan never materialized, for the precocious youth who created that sophisticated gown for his mother was determined to pursue a path in some aspect of art, and voiced his intention of doing so. Fashion was Erté's lifelong passion, and his interest in it may have

begun when, as a child, he stood by the side of his mother, Natalia, as she planned each social season's new wardrobe. The two would often visit the fashionable Nevsky Prospekt together, to see the current creations of the celebrated Russian *couturière*, Nadezhda Lamanova, then continue on to Morskaya Street, to inspect the latest millinery tidbits by the acclaimed French hatmaker, Alexandrine. If nothing tickled their fancy on their shopping forays, Erté and his mother would pore over the latest copies of *Damski Mir*, *Le Moniteur de la Mode* and *Les Modes*, the popular Russian and French fashion journals of the day, to find the ideal ensemble for their live-in seamstress to render into reality.

As the years progressed, Erté gradually incorporated more of his own frills and furbelows into these designs for his mother and, quite often, they were influenced by his immediate visual world. Many of his inspirations were merely extrapolations of works by contemporary couturiers and remain hard to distinguish from them; others were more unique, and suggested the quiet dignity

and flat, linear language of the icons that were ever-present in his Russian Orthodox world; still others hinted at the refinement, rhythmic movements and bold designs and colors of the same Persian miniatures that intrigued his father, who collected books on them. Erté's visits to the Hermitage Museum also left their mark upon his work. The geometric, floral and interlace patterns, and the use of silver, copper and gold, are reminiscent of that great institution's Turkish majolica collection, while his elegant and delicate line, balance and symmetry suggest the illustrations of Attic vases that he analyzed for hours. His designs grew gradually more elaborate and flamboyant as a result of his exposure to the Imperial Ballet and Opera productions presented in turn-of-the-century St Petersburg.

In fact, the young Erté found the colors, lines and light of the stage worlds created by such artists-cum-designers at Léon Bakst, Konstantin Korovin and Alexandre Benois so dynamic, opulent and mesmerizing, that he immediately started to collect postcards of the costumed

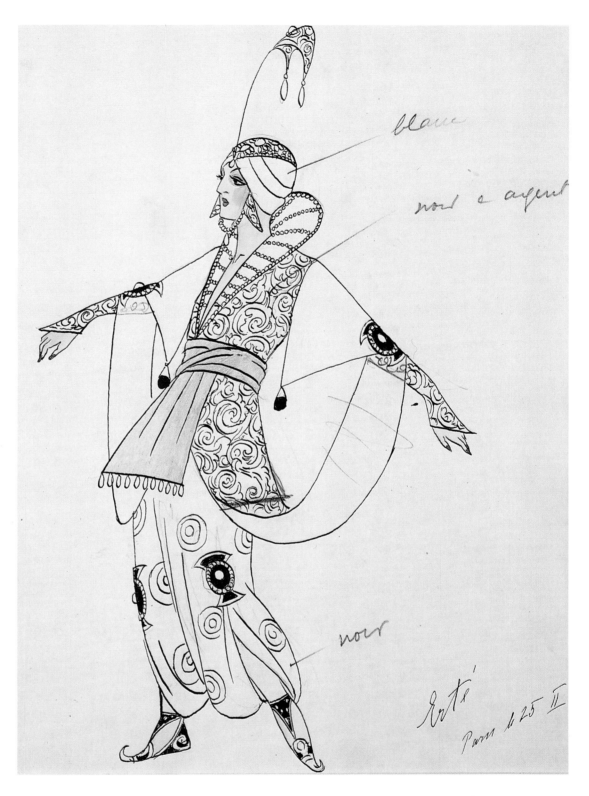

dancers and divas, so that he could refresh his memory
of the productions and then create his own ballets and
operas, along with their appropriate costumes and sets,
as an imaginative exercise.

With such an evident artistic prodigy on her hands,
Madame Tirtoff believed that her son would benefit from
master instruction, so she arranged for Erté to take
lessons from Ilya Repin (1844-1930), the great Russian
realist painter at the Imperial Academy of Fine Arts.
According to Erté, these elective courses 'left little
(stylistic) impact' on him, but they did emphasize the
essential elements of line and proportion that he would
always apply to his work thereafter.

Much of his initial output was executed as a personal

challenge, and as the years progressed in St Petersburg,
Erté's talent became as obvious as was his determination
to work as a fashion illustrator in Paris, the undisputed
fashion capital of the world. His father eventually
consented, and allowed his son to move to the City of
Light the year after he graduated from Kronstadt College
in 1911.

Erté moved to Paris in 1912, where the 19-year-old
found getting work more difficult than he had
anticipated. Although he had boundless ambition and
ability, he had neither professional experience nor
contacts. He worked initially under his new *nom de
plume* as the foreign-based fashion illustrator of the St
Petersburg monthly, *Damski Mir*, but a full year passed

before he finally secured a position at Maison Caroline, a small dressmaking firm that he soon discovered was a copy house which pirated the collections of the fine couture concerns. One of many such operations in Paris, Maison Caroline sent its representatives covertly to the showings of the important designers, where their innovative offerings were scrutinized, and then sketched from memory, patterned, assembled and sold. Such thievery was unconscionable to Erté and, in order to avoid it, he drew variations rather than exact duplications of the recently reviewed ensembles. His creative flair got him discharged from Caroline after less than a month, but hired immediately by Paul Poiret; the pre-eminent couturier recognized the parallels with his own work, and the promise of more exciting designs from this young artist.

Many of the pre-World War I renderings which Erté created for Poiret displayed the same line, rhythm and color that his new employer had so admired in Léon Bakst's 1908 Russian Ballet costumes and he continued to incorporate them into his own creations; others reflected Erté's strong theatrical bent, which Poiret utilized almost at once, instructing Erté to produce adaptations of his more exotic creations for certain select patrons. With the success of these designs, Erté progressed rapidly from modifying old ideas to devising new costumes for the Poiret's distinctive 'Rose Label.'

Erté remained at Chez Poiret for 18 months, and this period was crucial to the development of his fashion sensibility and illustrative style. As he worked closely with the *premières* – the seamstresses who made the ensembles for clients – he came to understand the principles of costume construction, and how his designs could be rendered into reality through the use of the appropriate textiles, cloth cuts and supporting seams. As a result of sketching Poiret's and his own ideas for magazine reproduction, his artistic style matured as well. Most of these assignments called for black-and-white designs, which required the use of pen and India ink, and resulted in a technique that, according to the artist, 'developed rapidly and became very precise with extremely fine lines. I got to the point,' he added, 'of using Gillot Number 3000 – the finest nib made.'

In addition to his fashion work for Poiret, Erté assisted the designer in developing outrageous costumes for the firm's *au courant* clients to wear to the staged masquerade balls which were then in vogue. Such costume balls interested the artist personally, because he also liked to attend them wearing his own ensembles, which often became the talking point of these events. To the Grand Prix Bal d'Opéra of 1914 – which was chronicled as being one of the most visually spectacular affairs – Erté wore a form-fitting silver lamé costume, complete with pearl wings and ebony-plumed cap, that caused quite a sensation. Sensational, too, was the consensus opinion of his costume for another ball: a

ABOVE
Knitting bag of interwoven ribbons for *Harper's Bazaar*. 1918.

RIGHT
Portrait of Lina Cavalieri. 1914.

diamond-studded body suit whose gold lamé cape was lined with freshly-picked red roses which were also strewn on the ground upon entry.

Such frivolities ended with the onset of World War I, as did the opportunities for Erté to work directly for Poiret's clients, when the master couturier closed his house in August 1914. In the same month Erté moved to Monaco, where he hoped to continue his fashion-illustration career. The artist decided that a United States-based publication would provide him with the best opportunity to succeed in this area – America was far removed from the war, was prosperous, and its small yet well-traveled readership was a group with which he had got on well in Paris. Following such logic, Erté devised an illustration for an imaginative cover designed to appeal to such an audience, and then flipped a coin to determined whether to submit it to *Harper's Bazaar* or *Vogue*. *Harper's* won the toss, and six months after the artist had submitted his rendering of 'Schéhérézade' to the magazine, the design graced its cover, marking the start of his 22-year-long affiliation with the publisher.

LEFT
Erté poses in his own Clair de
Lune costume design, Monte
Carlo, 1920.

RIGHT
Erté with his longterm
companion, Prince Nicholas, in
1920.

His cover designs for *Harper's* soon became successful, and Erté began to contribute illustrations to the magazine, featuring the chic costumes that were 'seen on the streets' of Monte Carlo. His original designs for coats, dresses, handbags, parasols and fans soon replaced these, and the editorials described them as 'the stuff of dreams,' that could 'adorn any woman's charm.'

Erté was becoming increasingly well known, and on the strength of this Henry Bendel and B. Altman in New York contracted him to produce seasonal lines of sport and evening wear. Smart, stunning and sumptuous, the costumes that he created from 1915 to 1918 displayed the Continental style that most American *mondaines* demanded in their wardrobes.

At the same time that Erté was making a name for himself in fashion illustration in the United States, he was commissioned to create a number of costumes for the prominent Romanian actor, Edward de Max, for his comedy role in the satire, *La Fête de St-Cyr*. De Max, who was Sarah Bernhardt's leading man, and who had met and admired Erté's theatrical work while the artist was at Chez Poiret, was just as delighted with his resultant Third-Republic court-jester and *le coq* ensembles as was Benédicte Rasmini, the highly respected music-hall proprietress/producer. She accordingly in 1916 engaged Erté to design the costumes for two tableaux in her forthcoming revues at the Théâtres Michel and Fémina: *Vilbert-Panachot le Dictateur* and *Les Amazones à Travers les Siècles*. Erté's extravagant elaborations of contemporary fashions were highlights of the former production, while exotic Near-Eastern and European historical court costumes held sway in the latter. Eight additional commissions followed within a short period of time, and their success brought Erté private contracts to design the stage ensembles for Mistinguette and Gaby Deslys, the two top music-hall divas of the day.

The artist also attracted the attention of Max Weldy, the incomparable costume-maker whose Parisian workshop produced the costumes, décor and curtains for the most important theater productions in Paris, Beirut, Barcelona, Calcutta, Hong Kong, and New York. As a result of Weldy's recommendation, Erté was asked to design the costumes and décor for two tableaux at the Folies-Bergère in 1919. These were entitled *Venise au XVIII Siècle* and *Fond de la Mer*, and Erté's exotic *commedia dell'arte* characters and deep-sea creature concoctions were hailed as the stars of these productions, and marked the start of the artist's 12-year association with the Folies-Bergère.

During this golden age of the music hall, Erté's designs delighted New York audiences as well, for such stellar American producers as George White, Irving Berlin and Florenz Ziegfeld traveled to Europe to contract the artist to create the daring, near-naughty sets and costumes that their respective *Scandals*, *Music Box Revue* and *Follies* demanded. According to contemporary reviews, Erté's work attained the recognition he desired, some critics citing the 'gasps of wonderment' from the audience, others commenting on the costumes themselves

LEFT
Erté in 1925 in his Hollywood
studio with one of the costumes
he designed for the 'Oriental
Ballet' sequence in the MGM
movie *Paris* (released 1929).

RIGHT
Carmel Myers wears the costume
Erté designed for her for the
1926 movie version of *Ben Hur*.

as 'breathtaking in their grandeur.' According to one pithy account, 'there were large quantities of gorgeous costumes, much of them on the chorus from the neck up and the shoes down.' Indeed, many of the artist's designs for the music hall were specifically meant for near-nude dancers, and whenever he was given the task of creating them, he admitted to following two simple principles: 'the first was to find one detail (a hairstyle, a piece of jewelry or some other accessory) which was sufficiently interesting or striking to suggest the idea for a costume; the second was to build a costume by extending the lines of the naked body into decorative arabesques.'

Whether it was to be brief, or called for more cover, every costume that Erté created for the chorines in these productions was as sensible as it was sensational. For ease of movement, costumes were as lightweight as

possible: spangles often served in place of beads; printed cloth gave similar visual effects to those of heavily-woven brocades or damasks, while feathers were judiciously used in lieu of furs. To withstand the stress of hard wear and constant handling, each costume was durably constructed with stretchable cloth and reinforcing seams.

Although these were among the more startling costumes that crossed the stage, Erté's designs for the theatrical corps were generally the last that he created once a contract to design a revue was in hand. Separate act settings and, when necessary, curtains, were initially conceived and, as Erté's 51 chronologically logged illustrations for a 1920 production of *Les Rois des Légende* indicate, the main character costumes in each act were designed after their décor, and these were then followed by the usually scanty, auxiliary-role costumes.

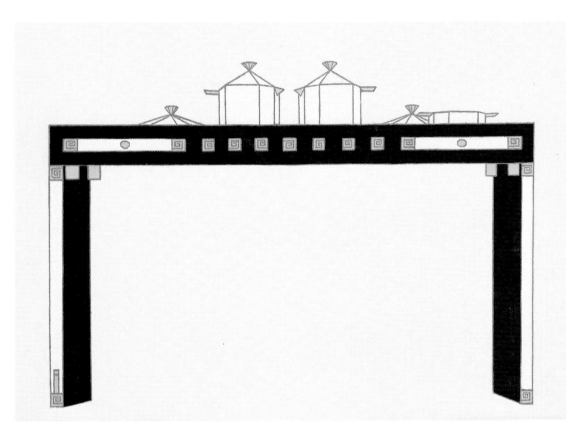

LEFT
Table design for the Paris
magazine *Art et Industrie*, for
which Erté produced a number
of cover designs and illustrations
on his return from the USA in
1926.

BELOW
Fan umbrellas, 1922, an
illustration for *Harper's Bazaar*.
Erté signed his first ten-year
contract with the magazine in
1915 and continued to work for
Harper's for 22 years.

FAR RIGHT
Tête de Mannequin IV, 1930.

In addition to the daring visual element of his designs,
Erté was also responsible for numerous theatrical
innovations. Among these were 'living curtains' of
elaborately beplumed and bejeweled dancers, who
appeared to float before the limelight, and 'costumes
collectifs,' which were single costumes that were shared
by a group of performers.

Erté was quick to admit that the years immediately
following the Armistice comprised his first great
professional period; he was successful, well-respected,
and his designs – especially for the stage – were in

demand on both sides of the Atlantic. Visiting divas,
prima ballerinas and impresarios sought him out to
contract him to create elegant costumes to glamorize
their roles. In 1920 the soprano Mary Garden asked the
artist to design a sumptuous wardrobe for her lead in the
Chicago Opera Company's production of *L'Amore dei
Tre Re*, Montemezzi's tragic story set in tenth-century
Italy. The aspiring diva Ganna Waleska commissioned
him to design a series of costumes for her appearances in
I Pagliacci, *Manon*, *Tosca* and *Rigoletto*. Serge Diaghilev
likewise asked Erté to submit designs for *The Sleeping*

Beauty, a ballet which eventually arrived onstage in 1922.

The nascent American film industry, which drew most of its early stars from the stage, also called upon Erté with offers of work as a costume designer. His first contract was with William Randolph Hearst's motion-picture company, Cosmopolitan Productions, for a scene in the silent-screen movie, *The Restless Sex*, which starred Marion Davies. The nearly 40 designs that Erté created for this mythologically-based Greco-Egyptian-Indian '*Bal des Arts*' sequence were astounding in their detail, and were described as 'brilliant' and 'lavish.' One reviewer wrote that: 'The Ball of the Gods was the most magnificent ballroom scene ever done in motion pictures.'

While this might have been an enjoyable intellectual exercise in design for Erté, his illustrations for both fashion and follies kept him at work in Paris for four years, before a serious invitation to work in Hollywood was extended by Louis B. Mayer, the Russian-born chief of Metro-Goldwyn-Mayer. The idea of working full-time in a new medium that could influence style trends globally was an exciting challenge for Erté, and when it was coupled with Mayer's proposed theme for the first movie, about the life of a celebrated Parisian fashion designer, the artist was so personally flattered that he accepted the offer and moved to Hollywood in 1925. This *roman à clef*, entitled *Paris*, was neither written nor produced immediately, however; the studio decided to delay the project in favor of applying the artist's talents to such productions as *Ben Hur*, *The Mystic*, *Dance Madness*, *Bright Lights*, *Time*, *The Comedian* and *La Bohème*.

Except for the historical *Ben Hur* and *La Bohème*, the films that demanded Erté's attention were the light, jazz-age 'flapper films' that pleased American audiences at this time. Usually teamed with Robert Z. Leonard – who also directed *The Restless Sex* for Cosmopolitan – and the set designer Cedric Gibbons – who later designed the famous Oscar statuette – Erté extended his six-month MGM contract and remained in Hollywood to work for one year. But by the end of that period he had become 'utterly disillusioned' with the American movie capital. He didn't agree with the peculiar design demands that various stars placed upon what were meant to be period costumes; he was restricted by the tight time schedules that producers allowed for the redesign and execution of script rewrites; he disliked the too rustic air of Los Angeles. His lifestyle weighed heavily upon Erté; he became depressed and longed for the more cosmopolitan Europe and the recognition that was accorded to him there. The artist therefore rejected his next studio contract with MGM and returned to Paris to re-establish himself as the king of the Continental revue designers, anticipating the personal sense of achievement that this goal promised.

His re-entry was initially difficult. Erté had presented himself so suddenly in a field where so many others now practiced, that he received few initial commissions for the French stage. He designed the costumes and sets for some Folies-Bergère productions, but the majority of his work continued to come from America. George White relied solely upon his talents to create the costumes and décor for his extravagant musical comedy, *Manhattan Mary* (1927), and all the tableaux for his yearly editions of the 'Scandals'. The diva Lucrezia Bori engaged him to design an elaborate wardrobe for her appearance with the New York Metropolitan Opera. Apart from the stage, Erté also accepted his second ten-year contract with *Harper's Bazaar*.

Erté's unchanging fashion style did not comply completely with that of the late 'Roaring Twenties' *Bazaar* readership, and the editors of the publication asked Erté to create rather more nebulous cover designs, which nowadays seem to suggest a Cubist inspiration. This was a style that differed dramatically from his illustrations for the short stories and novellas that appeared simultaneously in *Fémina*, *Cosmopolitan* and *L'Illustration*; the latter were exotic, other-worldly and far removed from the utilitarian designs for lamps, chairs and tables that he created as a 'complete change' for *Art et Industrie*, the respected design journal of the day.

In 1929, Erté's reputation brought him two extraordinary commissions from New York, which he accepted enthusiastically: one was from the *Encyclopedia Britannica* to write a discourse on the evolution of contemporary dress for its fourteenth edition; the second came from the Amalgamated Silk Corporation to design

LEFT

Erté continued to take on new design contracts in the 1920s and 1930s, in addition to his work for the stage. This design for Holeproof Hosiery dates from 1931.

RIGHT

Design for a lace dress, 1937.

ALLURE

Because of its sheer delicacy . . . its enchanting colors . . . its satisfying durability . . . Holeproof Hosiery has an irresistible allure for the woman whose discriminative sense leads her instinctively to the beautiful.

HOLEPROOF HOSIERY

Holeproof Hosiery Company, 1107 Broadway, New York   Holeproof Hosiery Company of Canada, Limited, London, Canada

15 pattern collections for silks, tapestries and wall coverings. The former established the artist as both a literary as well as an artistic authority on fashion, while the latter, which saw the eventual production of 200 designs for the textile industry, proved to be the commercial success that opened the door to Erté's subsequent design contracts with Holeproof Hosiery, Delman Shoes and Decca Records, among others.

Throughout this period, the artist's logbooks indicate that he had indeed become one of the most prominent costume and stage designers in Paris. Paul Derval, the director of the Folies Bergère , relied on Erté's creativity to produce the sumptuous look of such productions as *Princesses de Légende* and *Les Parfums*. So, too, did

those who were involved in the production of dramatic and comedy stage productions. The writer-cum-actor Sacha Guitry asked the artist to contribute a number of fashion designs to clothe the cast of his play, *Lindberg*, which came hot on the heels of the aviator's recent transatlantic flight; the actor-director Harry Baur likewise engaged Erté to draw up all of the designs for *La Princesse Lointaine*, a neo-Romantic comedy about a lovelorn crusader prince.

La Princesse Lointaine (1929) was a personal milestone in the artist's stage-design career because it was the first time that he was asked to create the entire visual look for a Parisian production. By now the European producers and directors understood that Erté's costumes and sets could convey their desired illusion, as well as being practical to produce and comfortable for their actors to carry and change; it was therefore not surprising that this Continental commission came from a man who once wore one of Erté's costumes. In fact, that particular costume was one of the artist's first: a Near-Eastern robe which was created in 1913 when Erté was still at Chez Poiret. This design accompanied another for an exotic, wired-tunic pyjama ensemble, which Erté crafted for the notorious Mata Hari in *Le Minaret* and which was among those which were hailed by *The New York Times* fashion correspondent as having 'set Europe by the ears,' in that it 'revolutionized the silhouette' of fashion in prewar Europe.

Much of the equally sensational work which Erté went on to create for the non-musical stage was, like his output for *Le Minaret*, adapted from historical costumes, and was very much in vogue with what theatergoers wanted to see at the time. During the first few decades of the twentieth century, stage design tended to be more symbolic rather than realistic in its approach – a preference shown in such overwhelmingly popular productions as Max Reinhardt's *Sumurnun* and d'Annunzio's *La Pisanelle de la Morte*.

The remote Near East and Levant were particularly prevalent settings for many of the productions on which Erté worked, as is evident from titles such as *Aphrodite* and *The Secret of the Sphinx* that appear in his records. Best-selling novels, including the intriguing works of the travel-and-romance writer Pierre Loti, often influenced the selection of such locales, as did current events throughout the 1920s, like Howard Carter's discovery of the tomb of Tutankhamen in the Valley of the Kings.

During the 1930s and into the 1940s, Erté was increasingly involved with theatrical design and, to a diminishing degree, with fashion illustration. He had signed his second ten-year contract with *Harper's Bazaar* in 1926, and continued to contribute designs to the magazine, but in 1932 Carmel Snow, the former fashion editor of its rival publication *Vogue*, assumed the top editorial position at *Harper's*, and she – according to Erté – 'not only wanted to supervise my work, but to impose her own ideas' upon it. Since he had never encountered such regulation before, the artist was taken aback, yet he still complied by submitting prospective cover sketches from which Ms Snow could then select. Numbering an astounding 200 in all, these were not sketches as much as beautifully-executed miniature paintings which, when chosen, were often used exactly as rendered for the publication.

In theatrical design much of his work during this period was for the music hall, an arena that was then experiencing a brief, post-Depression resurgence, and one that offered its patrons balletic productions in lieu of the former extravaganzas, which were underwritten by enormous budgets. Other commissions that the artist

received were for historically-based operettas, such as *Les Travaux d'Hercule*, *Au Temps des Merveilleuses*, *Les Joies du Capitole*, and *Amour Royal*, which dealt successively with Greek, Roman and First Republic times. Although it was contemporary rather than set in an earlier era, *It's in the Bag*, a revue staged in London at the Savile Theatre, was one of the most popular productions on which Erté worked at this time. 'Not even in Mr Cochran's great days have I seen a show more continuously beautiful to the eye,' wrote one reviewer, during a long run that helped Erté gain numerous other contracts from London impresarios to design shows at the Palladium and Hippodrome, among others.

With the onset of World War II and the German occupation of Paris, work for the foreign stage vanished completely. Erté continued to create designs for the Paris stage, but the conscientious designer was encumbered by numerous practical problems posed by the occupation and the ongoing war. Maintaining enough drawing paper and paint was initially difficult; his longer-standing challenge came in creating fanciful – yet workable – designs that didn't require excessive labor or the use of materials such as buttons, zippers and leather, all of which were either in short supply, severely rationed or

completely unobtainable. Erté overcame these obstacles,
as his sketches produced during this period indicate: his
costumes were now made of large, easy-to-cut geometric
pieces which required few seams and which were then
draped or pulled together by knotting or lacing the
various separate parts.

When the war ended and Paris was liberated, Erté was
contracted to create the sets and costumes for an
forthcoming production of Donizetti's opera, *Don
Pasquale* (1945). The success of the resulting
performance, and Erté's magnificent designs for the
eighteenth-century *commedia dell'arte* characters were
so highly regarded that the artist was asked to design the
costumes and stage sets for a different opera each year
over the next three years. *Les Mamelles de Tirésias*
(1947), a composition by Francis Poulenc, was the last of
this sequence, the sets of which one critic called
'exquisite fantasies.'

Throughout the late 1940s and into the 1950s, Erté
devised the designs for a number of shows at the
reopened Moulin Rouge, Narcissus and Folies-Pigalle
and leading revues in London, New York and Montreal.
But in North America the artist's workload was reduced
substantially because of the threat of the workers' strikes
which were then being staged by the newly-powerful
labor unions. With free time on his hands, Erté was able
to work on *The Alphabet*, a personal project that he had
begun in 1927, and to accept an important French
commission to design the costumes, décor and maquettes
for Giuseppe Verdi's *La Traviata* (1951).

Modeling operatic stage sets presented one of the major
creative demands of the artist's career, for not only did he
have physically to work in a third dimension, he also had
to learn the technical mechanics of the stage, their cost,
and the ways in which the proscenium could work. *La
Traviata* was successful, and its triumph assured Erté that
he could successfully apply his talents to anything. Over
the next decade he accepted fewer theatrical commissions,
in order to work on significant European operatic and
comic-operatic productions such as Debussy's *Pelléas et
Melisande* (1952), Mozart's *Cosí fan Tutti* (1952), and
Rameau's *Castor et Pollux* (1960). He then expanded into
opera-ballet and ballet films, contributing to such
productions as Roussel's *Padmâvati*, Ravel's *Mother Goose*
and Cuny's *Le Coiffeur-Miracle* (1960).

It may be that this new undertaking to create stage
maquettes had sparked Erté's desire to sculpt, for in the
early 1960s the artist traded in his gouache, brush, ink,
pen and paper, in favor of aluminum, copper, iron,
wood, glass, enamel and oils, and created a series of free-
form sculptures which he entitled 'formes picturales.'
Twenty years later he was still involved in the production
of a series of popular bronze sculptures which were
based upon his designs from the 1910s and 1920s.

Renewed interest in Erté's earlier works began to grow
in the mid-1960s, a full decade after the artist's career
had come to a near standstill. During the 1950s and into
the 1960s, Erté had exhibited occasionally, as well as
contributing to some revues, but by 1966 he had been
forgotten by most producers and directors. Although his
style was readily adaptable, the impresarios of the period
considered its proponent and his work as being of
another era.

to illustrate magazine covers, posters and books; and he became the focus of retrospectives at such major museums as the Metropolitan in New York and the Smithsonian Institution in Washington, D.C. Many prospective collectors who discovered Erté's work at these exhibitions were dismayed to find that a large number of the works which they wished to acquire were sold within moments of being placed on the market.

To satisfy this growing demand, especially in the United States, Erté was encouraged by his new agents to produce graphics. His first series of lithographs, *The Numerals*, was published in 1968 and gave elegant, feminine form to the numbers from zero to nine. *The Six Precious Stones*, *The Four Seasons* and *The Four Aces* were issued in the years that followed, and these were succeeded by the last of his single-subject lithographic productions. *The Alphabet* (1977), which was a spirited

ABOVE LEFT
Leo, horoscope design for *The London Sketch*, 1939.

BELOW LEFT
Maid of honor design, 1953.

ABOVE
Indian reporter design, *Wonderworld*, New York's World's Fair, 1964.

RIGHT
Cats and Owls shirt design, 1970.

This attitude changed dramatically less than a year later, due to a chance meeting between two artistic colleagues in London. This occurred at the Grosvenor Gallery when, at an enormously successful exhibition of drawings and pastels by the Art Nouveau artist Alphonse Mucha, Jacques Damase, the noted art historian, approached Eric Estorick, the gallery owner, and suggested that, since his promotion of Mucha was being so well received, his next logical move would be to reintroduce a certain artist who had worked during the heyday of Art Deco. The artist, of course, was Erté, whom Damase had recently come to know after working on a book about the music hall.

The day after that meeting, Eric and Salomé Estorick flew to Paris to meet the artist, resulting in a unique partnership between Erté, the celebrated designer, and Estorik, the marketing genius, which was to last over a quarter of a century. A series of single-artist exhibitions featuring Erté were organized by the Grosvenor Gallery and, within months, every one of these was sold out. Through the efforts of Estorick and his holding company, Sevenarts Ltd, which Erté now appointed as his exclusive agents, the artist received new commissions

26-piece series based upon the female form. Due to their overwhelming success, Erté was encouraged to apply his breathtaking designs to other multiple series, such as sculpture, jewelry and objets d'art among others, in which editions numbering 300 pieces would sell in a matter of weeks.

Many of these ideas developed during Erté's annual two-month holiday with the Estoricks at their home in Barbados. During this most productive of times, the prototypes for forthcoming multiple series were reviewed and revised; entrepreneurs from the United States and

Europe would visit to present projects to which they envisaged further applying Erté's exuberant lines; and the international itinerary for each forthcoming year was planned.

Although Erté was now in the autumn of his life, thanks to a chance meeting with the Estoricks, he now became one of the most prolific, successful, famed and fêted artists of the late twentieth century. A creative whirlwind whose enthusiasm for work seemed to grow greater with time, the artist at the age of 96 designed the complete stage sets and costumes for the Broadway

LEFT
Dancer's costume for the ballet *Ragtime* at the Ballet Théâtre, Angers (1974).

RIGHT
Erté in his 80s, still demonstrating his flair for exotic costume, and sporting an *Alphabet* design tiepin.

musical *Stardust*, and two sets for the Radio City Music Hall *Easter Show* (1988).

Erté's unexpected death on April 21, 1990, had been preceded six months earlier by that of his friend and confidante, Salomé Estorick, and was succeeded three years later by the death of her husband, Eric. The chapter closes, but the story continues by way of the original works and the multiple series produced by this most extraordinary individual who, when he was well into his nineties, apologized to a colleague for having lost his proficiency in Spanish, remaining fluent only in Russian, French, English and Italian.

The following selection of plates covers the period from 1911 – when the artist was deciding whether to sign his work with his family nicknames of 'Tir' or 'Pitch' – to 1988, by which time he was recognized and celebrated as 'Erté' for nearly eight decades of spectacular design work. Many of the illustrations emphasize Erté's contribution to the music hall, an area which comprised nearly 40% of the artist's total oeuvre. His work for fashion, opera and operetta are likewise prominent, for they constitute 50% of the artist's output of nearly 20,000 works. The drawings reproduced on the following pages were executed originally in India ink, or gouache and metallic paint, media that could convey the detail and descriptive fantasy in work which Erté admitted 'has been my mother, my wife, my friend, my mistress, my children, my life.'

Design for an Imaginary Ballet, 1911
Gouache, 16¼ × 20¼ inches (41.3 × 51.4 cm)

Loge de Théâtre, 1912
Gouache, 20¼ × 16¼ inches (51.4 × 41.3 cm)

ABOVE
Sports costume for Henri Bendel, 1915
Gouache, 15¼ × 12¼ inches (38.7 × 31.1 cm)

RIGHT
Dress for Henri Bendel, 1915
Gouache, 15¼ × 12¼ inches (38.7 × 31.1 cm)

LEFT
Costume design for La Belladonne, *Les Fleurs du*
Mal, 1917
Gouache, 10 × 6½ inches (25.4 × 16.5 cm)

ABOVE
Costume design for *Scaramouche,* **Folies-Bergère,**
1919
Gouache, 14¾ × 11¼ inches (37.5 × 28.6 cm)

Costume design for a Lantern-bearer in _Venise au_
XVIII Siècle, Folies-Bergère, 1919
Gouache, 18 × 11 inches (45.7 × 27.9 cm)

ABOVE
Costume design for the Shepherdess, _Les Rois des_
Légendes, Théâtre Fémina, Paris, 1919
Gouache, 14 × 11 inches (35.6 × 27.9 cm)

Set design for 'The King of Lahore', *Les Rois des*
Légendes, **Théâtre Fémina, Paris,** 1919
Gouache, 11 × 18 inches (27.9 × 45.7 cm)

**Costume design for the Adulteress, *Les Rois des
Légendes*, Théâtre Fémina, Paris**, 1919
Gouache, 12 × 10¼ inches (30.5 × 26 cm)

'New Bridges for the Seven Seas,' *Harper's Bazaar*
cover design, March 1919
Gouache, 22 × 15 inches (55.9 × 38.1 cm)

Costume design for Ganna Walska in *Tosca*, Act I,
Chicago Opera Company, 1920
Gouache, 11½ × 8 inches (29.2 × 20.3 cm)

Costume design for Ganna Walska in *Tosca*, Act III,
Chicago Opera Company, 1920
Gouache, 11½ × 8 inches (29.2 × 20.3 cm)

ABOVE
Costume design for the Chinese Empress in *La Dernière Nuit de Don Juan*, The Apollo, Paris, 1921
Gouache, 12½ × 12 inches (31.8 × 30.5 cm)

**Costume design for the Lilac Fairy in *The Sleeping
Beauty***, Diaghilev Ballet, 1921
Gouache, 20¼ × 16¼ inches (51.4 × 41.3 cm)

Costume design for Prince Charming in _The_
Sleeping Beauty, Diaghilev Ballet, 1921
Gouache, 20¼ × 16¼ inches (51.4 × 41.3 cm)

Les Trois Chemins. 1921
Gouache. 14 × 10½ inches (35.6 × 26.7 cm)

'Souvenirs,' *Harper's Bazaar* **cover design**. 1922
Gouache. 14¼ × 10⅝ inches (36.2 × 26.9 cm)

ABOVE AND RIGHT
Costume designs for Ganna Walska in *Manon*,
Chicago Opera Company, 1922
Gouache, 15¾ × 11⅜ inches (40 × 30 cm)

Costume design for the Princess of Indochina, *The*
Treasures of Indochina, L'Alcazar de Marseille, 1922
Gouache, 21½ × 29½ inches (54.6 × 74.9 cm)

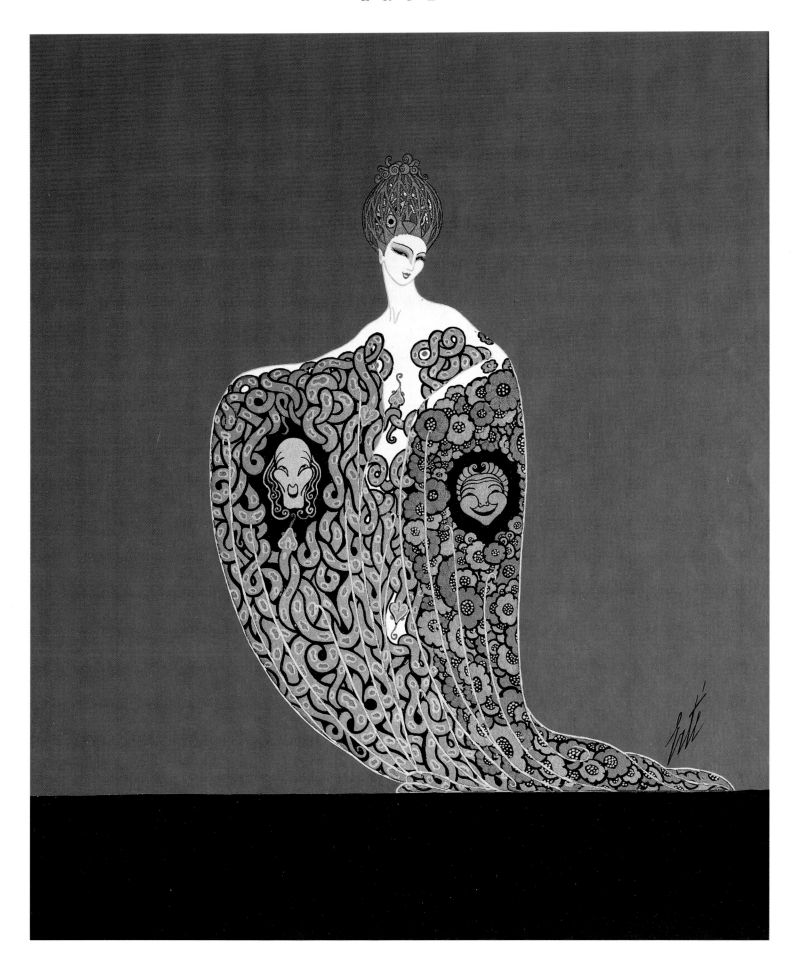

**Costume design for the Innocent and Morbid
Pleasures,** *The Treasures of Indochina,* 1922
Gouache, 12 × 9⅝ inches (30.5 × 24.4 cm)

**'Costumes pours les bals masqués: Arlequin,
Colombine, Pierrot,'** *Harper's Bazaar*, December
1922
Gouache, 9½ × 8¼ inches (24.1 × 20.9 cm)

ABOVE

**Costume design for Lotus, *The Treasures of
Indochina***, L'Alcazar de Marseille, 1922
Gouache, 20¼ × 16¼ inches (51.4 × 41.3 cm)

RIGHT

**Costume design for Mother of Pearl, *The Treasures
of Indochina***, L'Alcazar de Marseille, 1922
Gouache, 27¼ × 20¾ inches (69.2 × 52.7 cm)

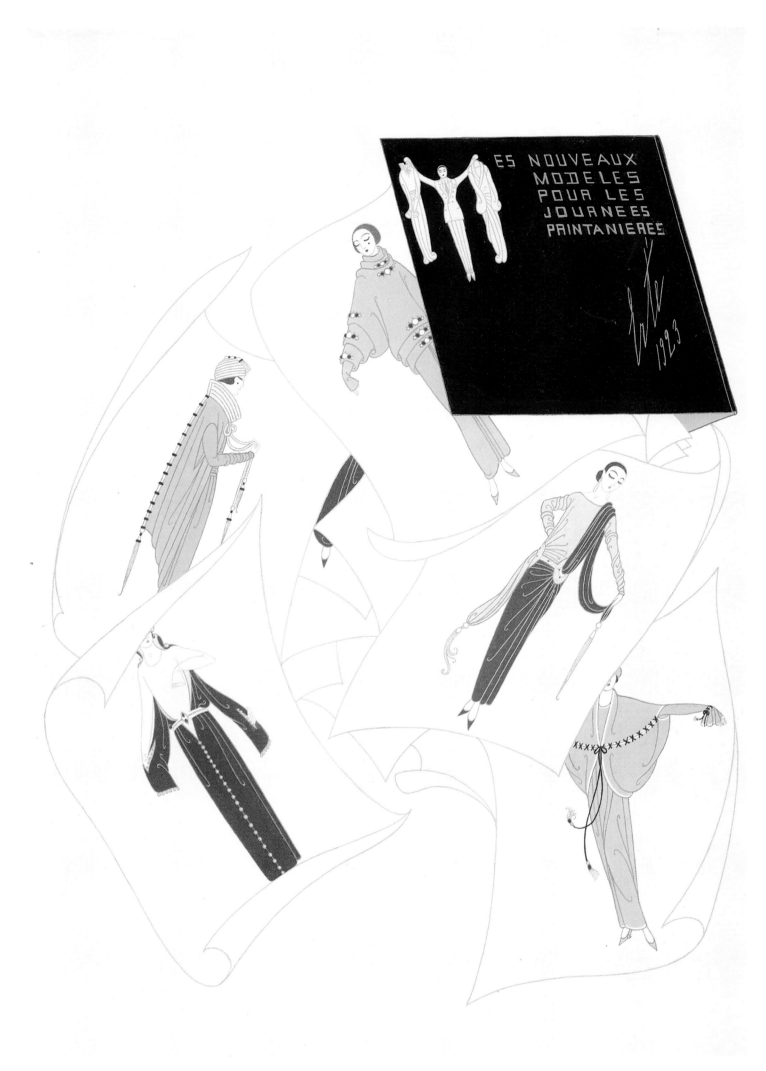

ES NOUVEAUX
MODELES
POUR LES
JOURNEES
PRINTANIERES

Erté
1923

'Aquarium,' *Harper's Bazaar* cover design, 1923
Gouache, 14 × 12 inches (35.6 × 30.5 cm)

LEFT
Five dress designs for *Harper's Bazaar*, 1923
Pen and ink, 12 × 8½ inches (30.5 × 21.6 cm)

51

ABOVE
Costume design for Ganna Walska as the Countess in *The*
***Marriage of Figaro*, Act II**, Chicago Opera Company, 1923
Gouache, 15½ × 11 inches (39.4 × 27.9 cm)

RIGHT
Costume design for the Diamond in *Les Pierres*
Précieuses, Folies-Bergère, Paris, 1923 and Irving
Berlin's *Music Box Revue*, New York, 1924
Gouache, 14 × 10½ inches (35.6 × 26.7 cm)

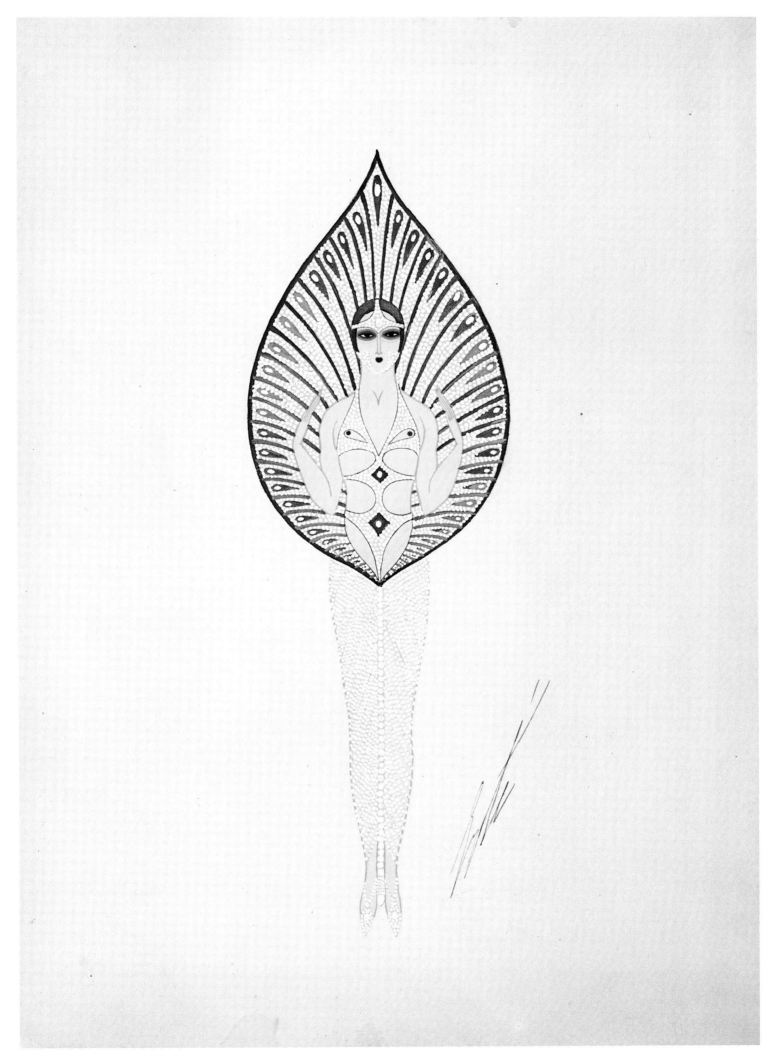

Triple costume design for the Baltic Sea, *Les Mers,*
George White's Scandals, New York, 1923
Gouache, 13⅜ × 18½ inches (34 × 47 cm)

Triple costume design for the Ocean, *Les Mers*,
George White's Scandals, New York, 1923
Gouache, 13⅜ × 18½ inches (34 × 47 cm)

LEFT

**Costume design for the East Wind, *Mah-Jongg*, Act
II**, George White's Scandals, New York, 1924
Gouache, 14⅞ × 10¾ inches (37.8 × 27.3 cm)

ABOVE

Costume design for Mah-Jongg, *Mah-Jongg*, George
White's Scandals, New York, 1924
Gouache, 14¾ × 10⅞ inches (37.5 × 27.4 cm)

ABOVE
Set design 'Décor-Paravent', _Mah-Jongg_, George
White's Scandals, New York, 1924
Gouache, 12½ × 15⅞ inches (31.7 × 40.1 cm)

RIGHT
Costume design for the South Wind, _Mah-Jongg_, Act 11,
George White's Scandals, New York, 1924
Gouache, 14¾ × 10⅞ inches (37.5 × 27.4 cm)

60

Triple costume design (center) for Golden Wedding,
Les Mariages, George White's Scandals, New York,
1924
Gouache, 15¼ × 11⅛ inches (38.7 × 28.5 cm)

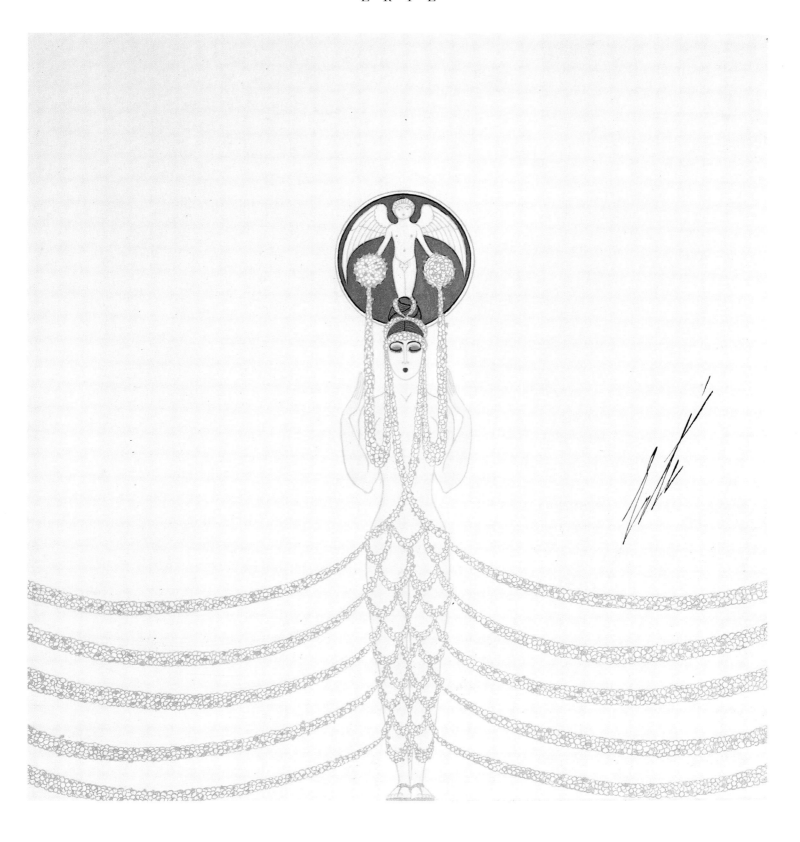

Triple costume design (center) for Marriage, *Les Mariages*, George White's Scandals, New York, 1924
Gouache, 15⅜ × 11⅜ inches (39.1 × 29 cm)

ABOVE
Silver and black curtain 'Deuxième Voile', *Les*
Mariages, George White's Scandals, New York, 1924
Gouache, 6¾ × 10⅜ inches (17.1 × 26.4 cm)

RIGHT ABOVE
Curtain design for 'The Oriental Ballet' in *Paris*,
MGM, designed 1925, film released 1929
Gouache, 11 × 16 inches (27.9 × 40.6 cm)

RIGHT BELOW
Curtain design (variation) for 'The Oriental Ballet'
in *Paris*, MGM, designed 1925, film released 1929
Gouache, 11 × 16 inches (27.9 × 40.6 cm)

Costume design for *Prince Amoureux*, George White's
Scandals, New York, 1925
Gouache, 15¼ × 11⅛ inches (38.7 × 28.4 cm)

'The Heat and the Clouds', *Harper's Bazaar* **cover
design**, July 1926
Gouache, 16 × 11½ inches (40.6 × 29.2 cm)

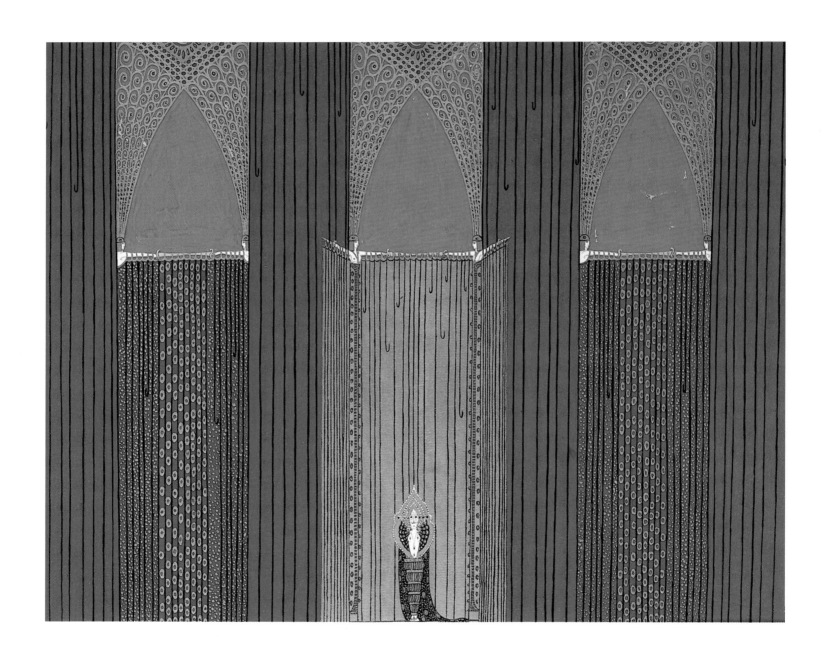

Set design for *The Golden Fables*, George White's
Scandals, New York, 1926
Gouache, 10¾ × 14¼ inches (27.3 × 36.2 cm)

**Costume design for the Gold of the Rhine Narrators
in *The Golden Fables*,** George White's Scandals, New
York, 1926
Gouache, 15 × 11½ inches (38.1 × 29.2 cm)

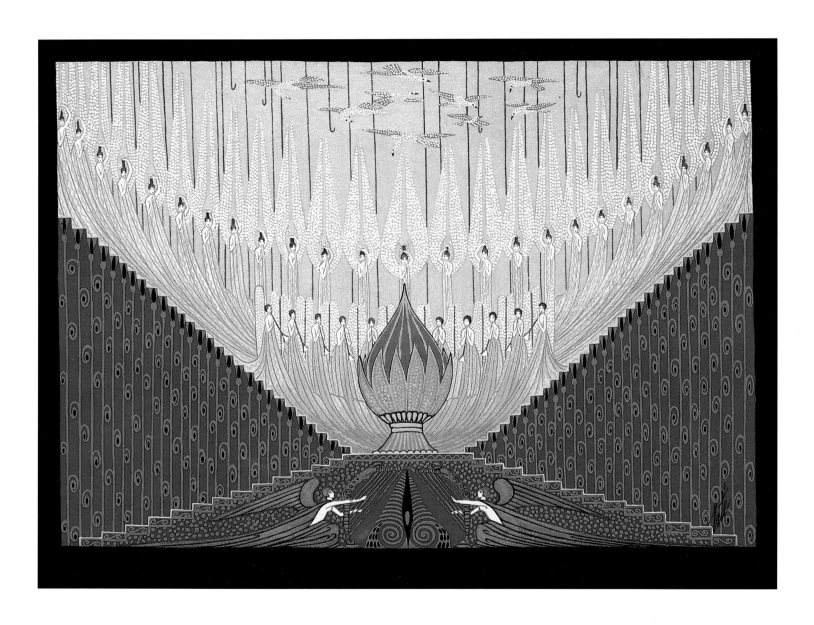

**Design for Finale, angels playing harps, trumpets
and lyres, *The Blues*, George White's Scandals, New
York, 1926**
Gouache, 11¼ × 15 inches (28.6 × 38.1 cm)

Angel Harpist costume design for *The Blues*, George
White's Scandals, New York, 1926
Gouache, 21¼ × 27½ inches (54 × 69.9 cm)

Costume design for *The Nile*, George White's Scandals,
New York, 1926
Gouache, 16¼ × 20¼ inches (41.3 × 51.4 cm)

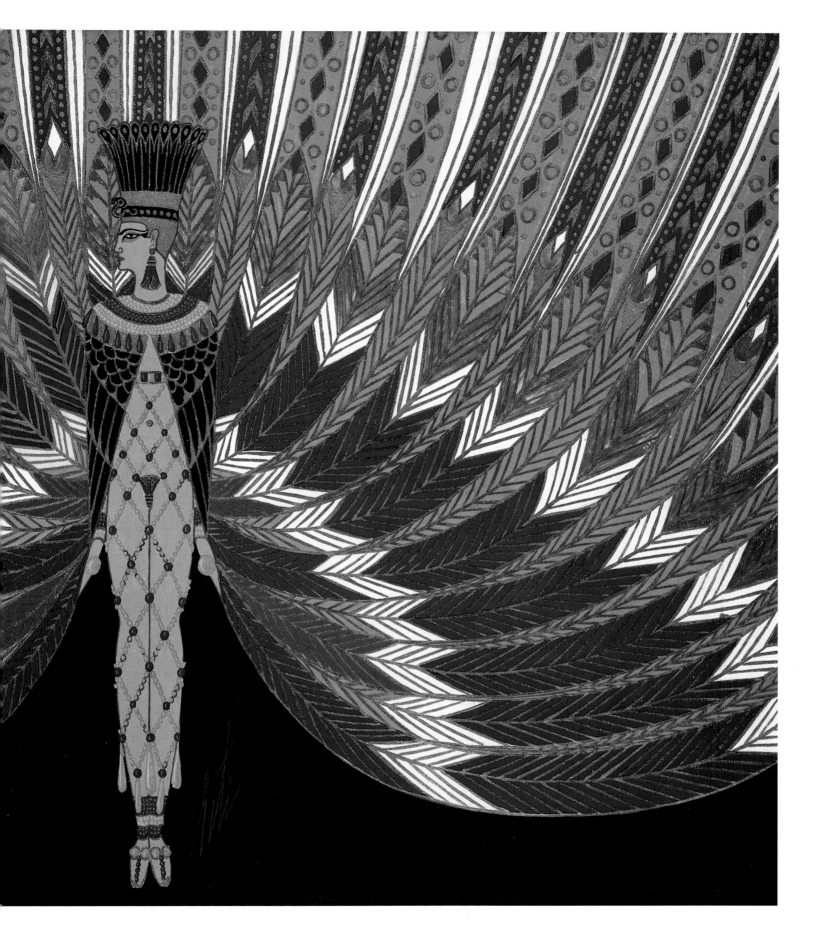

Set design for *The Spanish Scene*, George White's
Scandals, New York, 1926
Gouache, 11 × 15½ inches (27.9 × 39.4 cm)

ABOVE
'L'Hiver de la Femme (Vieillesse),' design for
International Cosmopolitan, 1927
Gouache, 11 × 11 inches (27.9 × 27.9 cm)

RIGHT
'Riviera', *Harper's Bazaar* cover design, Christmas
1927
Gouache, 15¾ × 11¾ inches (40 × 29.8 cm)

76

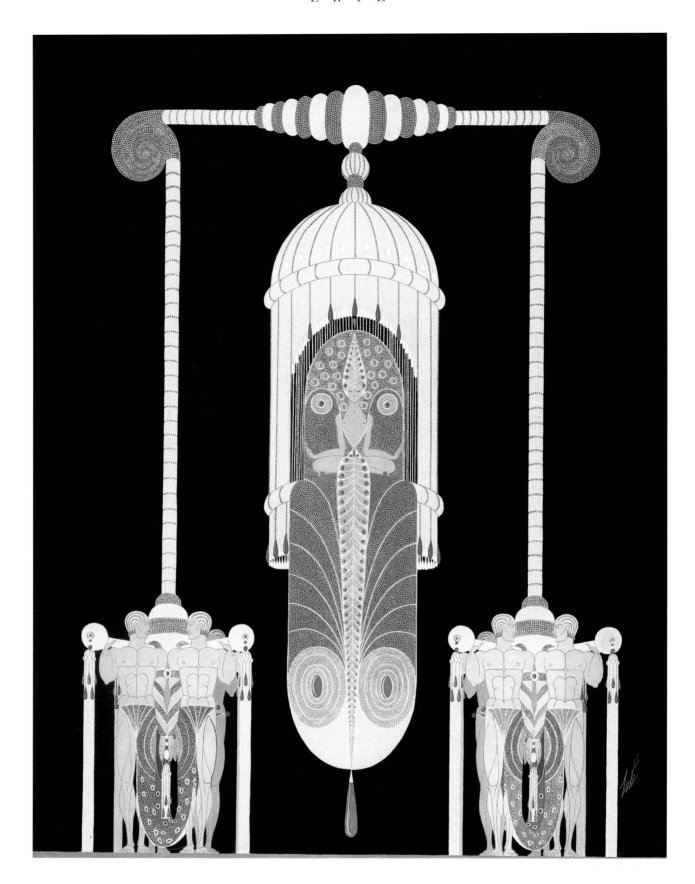

ABOVE
Costume design for the Attendants in *Les Pierreries*, Folies-
Bergère, Paris and George White's Scandals, New York, 1927
Gouache, 24 × 18 inches (61 × 45.7 cm)

RIGHT
Costume design for the Attendants in *Les Pierreries*, Folies-
Bergère, Paris and George White's Scandals, New York, 1927
Gouache, 22 × 13¾ inches (55.9 × 34.9 cm)

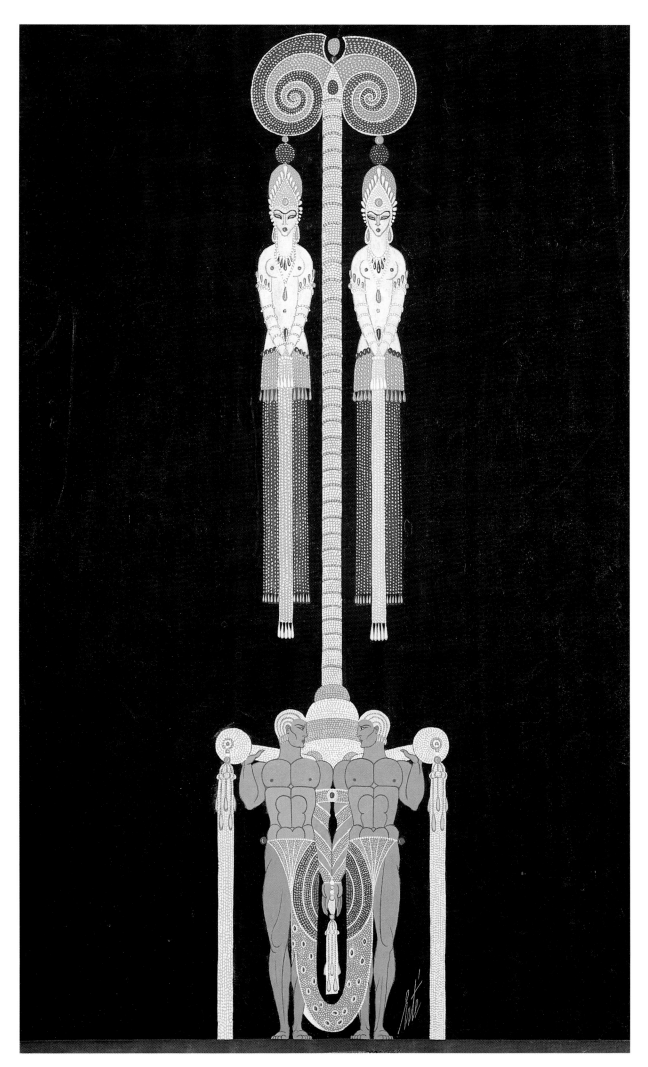

Costume design for Mélisande, *Pelleas et Mélisande*,
Metropolitan Opera Company, New York, 1927
Gouache, 15¾ × 11⅜ inches (40 × 28.9 cm)

RIGHT
**Costume design for an Exotic Bird in *L'Oiseau
Merveilleux*, Folies-Bergère, Paris, 1927**
Gouache, 22 × 14½ inches (55.9 × 36.8 cm)

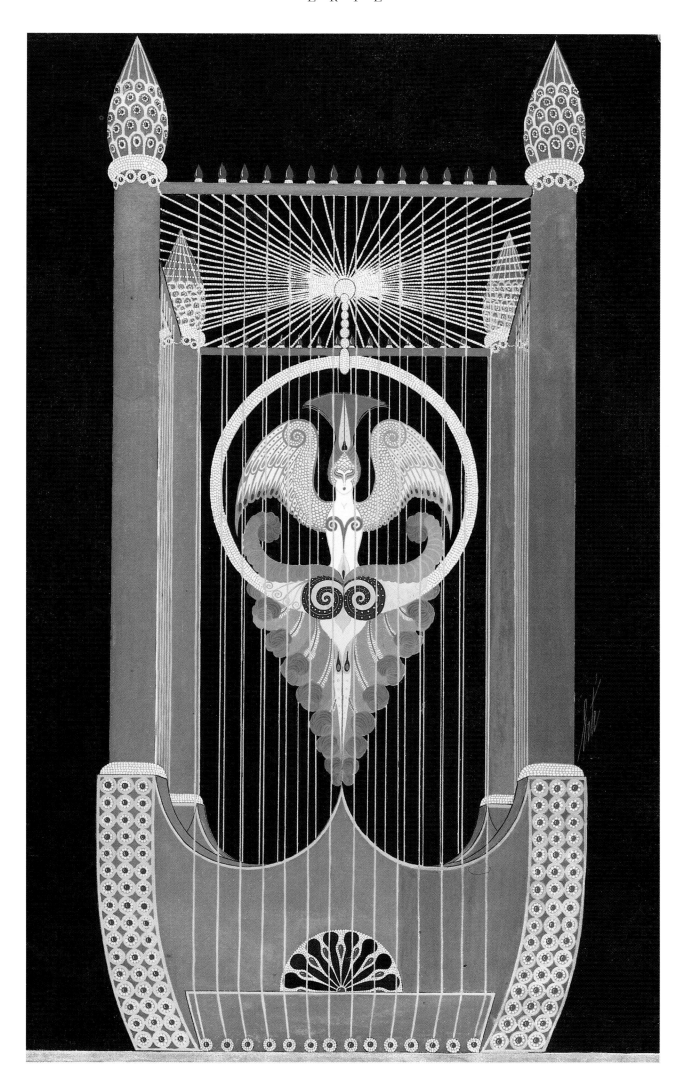

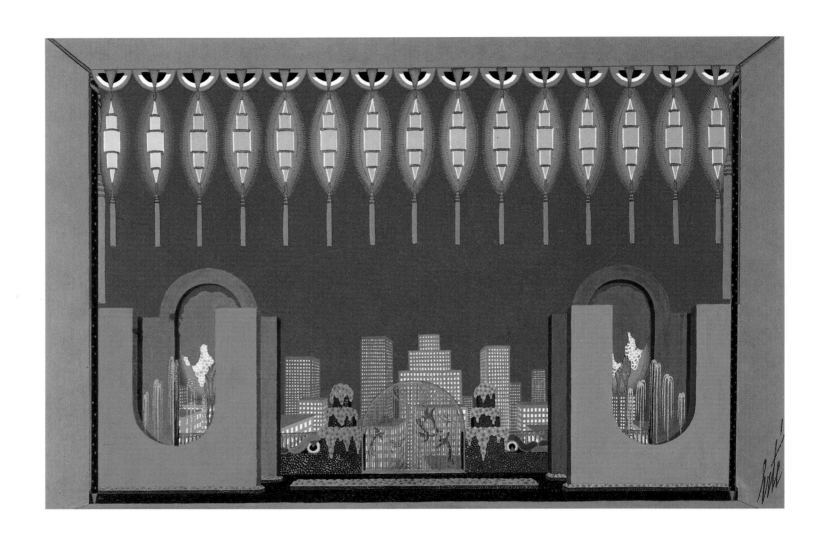

Set design for *Manhattan Mary*, Majestic Theater, New
York, 1927
Gouache, 9½ × 14⅛ inches (24.1 × 35.9 cm)

ABOVE LEFT

Design for beaded dress, *Manhattan Mary*, Majestic
Theater, New York, 1927
Gouache, 15⅛ × 11⅛ inches (38.4 × 28.2 cm)

ABOVE RIGHT

Design for yellow coat, *Manhattan Mary*, Majestic
Theater, New York, 1927
Gouache, 15⅛ × 10⅞ inches (38.4 × 27.6 cm)

'The Standard of Fashion', *Harper's Bazaar* **cover
design**, April 1928
Gouache, 14½ × 11 inches (36.8 × 27.9 cm)

ABOVE LEFT
Dress, hat and shoes designed for Davidow, New
York, 1928
Gouache, 15¼ × 11¼ inches (38.7 × 28.6 cm)

ABOVE RIGHT
Dress design for Davidow, New York, 1928
Gouache, 15¼ × 11¼ inches (38.7 × 28.6 cm)

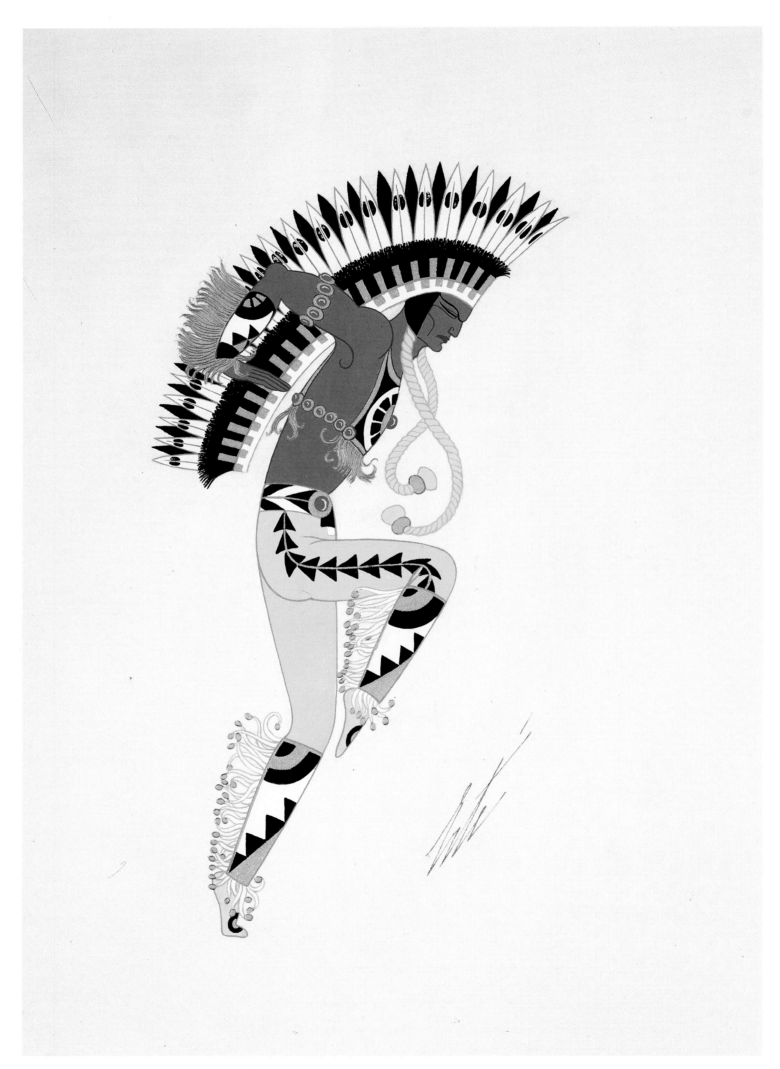

LEFT
Costume design for a Chief, *Indian Dagger Dance*,
George White's Scandals, New York, 1928
Gouache, 15¾ × 11¼ inches (40 × 28.6 cm)

ABOVE
Set design for *L'Arbre*, George White's Scandals, New
York, 1928
Gouache, 6⅞ × 9½ inches (17.5 × 24.1 cm)

87

LEFT
Curtain design for *Phantasm*, 1928
Gouache, 19⅝ × 12½ inches (49.8 × 31.7 cm)

ABOVE
'L'Arc en Ciel,' *Harper's Bazaar* cover design, 1929
Gouache, 15 × 11 inches (38.1 × 27.9 cm)

Wedding costume design for the Groom, *Aladdin,*
Folies Bergère, 1929
Gouache, 27¼ × 20¾ inches (69.2 × 52.7 cm)

ABOVE
La Grille de Porcelaine, *Aladdin,*
Folies Bergère, 1929
Gouache, 20¼ × 16¼ inches (51.4 × 41.3 cm)

***Mouvements divers* textile design**, 1930
Gouache, 20¼ × 16¼ inches (51.4 × 41.3 cm)

Illustration for short story 'The Sultan's Past,'
***Harper's Bazaar*, 1930**
Gouache, 15 × 11 inches (38.1 × 27.9 cm)

ABOVE
Costume design for Casanova, _Les Amoureux_, 1930
Gouache, 14½ × 10¾ inches (36.8 × 27.3 cm)

RIGHT
Paris Openings, _Harper's Bazaar_ cover design,
March 1931
Gouache, 16 × 12 inches (40.6 × 30.5 cm)

Red pump designed for Delman Shoes, New York,
1934
Gouache, 16 × 12 inches (40.6 × 30.5)

ABOVE
Design for coral earrings, 1932
Gouache, 11 × 9 inches (27.9 × 22.9 cm)

Costume design for Scots girl, *Ballet d'Enfants,* 1934
Gouache, 15 × 11 inches (38.1 × 27.9 cm)

Red dress designed for Les Coardes, *Au Pays de*
Sourire, 1934
Gouache, 14¾ × 11 inches (37.5 × 27.9 cm)

Harper's Bazaar cover design, February 1935
Gouache, 20¼ × 16¼ inches (51.4 × 41.3 cm)

RIGHT
Costume design for *Can Can*, Bal Tabarin, 1936
Gouache, 20¼ × 16¼ inches (51.4 × 41.3 cm)

LEFT
Aztec Ballet costume design, _It's in the Bag_, Saville
Theatre, London, 1937
Gouache, 16¼ × 20¼ inches (41.3 × 51.4 cm)

ABOVE
**Costume design for _Carmen_, Act 111 (second
version)**, 1937
Gouache, 15 × 11 inches (38.1 × 27.9 cm)

'Seagulls,' *Harper's Bazaar* cover design, July 1938
Gouache, 14½ × 11 inches (36.8 × 27.9 cm)

Costume design for Russian Peasant, *Tabarin*, 1938
Gouache, 14½ × 10½ inches (36.8 × 26.7 cm)

Set design for *Mariage à Trois*, 1940
Gouache, 10½ × 15 inches (26.7 × 38.1 cm)

Set design for the Pharoah's Palace, *Joseph*, 1943
Gouache, 10½ × 14½ inches (26.7 × 36.8 cm)

Set design for *Valentin*, Scene 3, 1945
Gouache, 10½ × 15 inches (26.7 × 38.1 cm)

LEFT BELOW
Set design for *Valentin*, Scene 4, 1945
Gouache, 10½ × 15 inches (26.7 × 38.1 cm)

ABOVE
Amazon costume design for *Biedermeier*, 1945
Gouache, 20¼ × 16¼ inches (51.4 × 41.3 cm)

Harlequin costume design for *Don Pasquale*, Palais
de Chaillot, 1945
Gouache, 27¾ × 20¾ inches (69.2 × 52.7 cm)

ABOVE
Design for window display, 1948
Gouache, 16¼ × 20¼ inches (41.3 × 51.4 cm)

LEFT
Set design for *Machinerie*, The Tabarin, Paris, 1948
Gouache, 15 × 10 inches (38.1 × 25.4 cm)

ABOVE
Set design for *Bolero*, 1950
Gouache, 15¼ × 12¼ inches (38.7 × 31.1 cm)

Set design for *The Kingdom of Toys*, Palladium
Theatre, London, 1949
Gouache, 6½ × 16 inches (16.5 × 40.1 cm)

LEFT
Costume design for Violetta, *La Traviata*, Paris
Opéra, 1951
Gouache, 15¼ × 10 inches (38.7 × 25.4 cm)

ABOVE
Costume design for a Girl, *La Traviata,* Paris Opéra,
1951
Gouache, 15¼ × 10 inches (38.7 × 25.4 cm)

Costume design for *El Val Sonada*, Teatro Espanol,
1955
Gouache, 11 × 9½ inches (27.9 × 22.9 cm)

Costume design for Dancers, Les Ombres Tristes,
Castor and Pollux, Lyons Festival, 1961
Gouache, 27¼ × 20¾ inches (69.2 × 52.7 cm)

y

ABOVE
Set design for Radio City Music Hall, 1961
Gouache, 11½ × 15 inches (27.2 × 38.1 cm)

RIGHT
Costume design for a Dancer, finale, *Flying Colours*,
Montreal Expo '67, 1967
Gouache, 20¼ × 16¼ inches (51.4 × 41.3 cm)

Design for Charnos stocking package, 1974
Gouache, 20¼ × 16¼ inches (51.4 × 41.3 cm)

ABOVE
Costume design for the Cakewalk soloist, *Ragtime*,
1975
Gouache, 11 × 9½ inches (29.2 × 24.1 cm)

Costume design for the Brigand Chief,
Schéhérezade, 1975
Gouache

Letter B from the *Alphabet* series, 1977
Gouache, 10 × 6½ inches (25.4 × 16.5 cm)

**Costume design for the Marschallin, Act 1, *Der
Rosenkavalier*,** Glyndebourne Opera Company, 1980
Gouache, 14¾ × 10¾ inches (37.5 × 27.5 cm)

Costume design for the Star, *Stardust*, 1988
Gouache, 14¾ × 10¾ inches (37.5 × 27.5 cm)

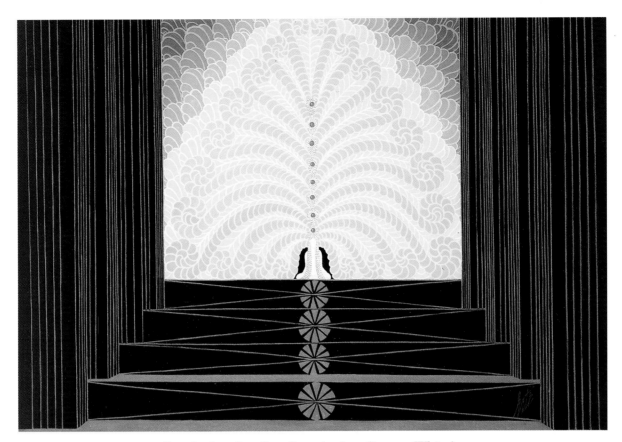

Set design for *Les Spectacles,* George White's
Scandals, 1928
Gouache, 11⅛ × 15¼ inches (28.25 × 38.7 cm)

ACKNOWLEDGMENTS

All illustrations are reproduced with the permission of
Sevenarts Ltd.